Fairy Boots

Tamsin Wood

Fairy Boots
Tamsin Wood

© Tamsin Wood 2015
All rights reserved. No part of this book can be reproduced or distributed in any form whatsoever without the permission of the author. The only exceptions are short quotations and some non-commercial uses allowed by copyright laws. All efforts have been made to make the contents as accurate as possible. However if there are inaccuracies the publisher cannot be held liable.

A CIP Record for this book can be found at the British Library.

Published with the assistance of Actual Books LTD.
Actualizeselfpublishing.com
Unit 19, 1 Green Street,
Eastbourne, East Sussex, BN21 1QN, UK

Cover design by Actual Books LTD.

Photography by Eileen Mason. eileenmason.co.uk

ISBN: Paperback: 978-0-9929046-5-4,

eBook: 978-0-9929046-6-1

Thanks to Eileen Mason Photography
for the beautiful illustrations,
Roberto do Falco and Silvia Hoefnagels
for their advice and encouragement,
and to my wonderful family who have
supported me throughout.
Xxxx

For my very own Master Thistleberry
and Miss Shimmersprite.
With love from Mummy
xx

And for Kelli Smith ...
Who inspired me to write this book.
Xx

Kelli Smith was born on 2nd January 2009. At just 3 months old she began to display symptoms of ill health and was diagnosed with Neuroblastoma a form of childhood Cancer. Despite scans, bone biopsies, chemotherapy and extensive surgery to remove abdominal tumours, Kelli relapsed after getting the all clear. Tragically there is no treatment protocol in place in the UK for relapsed Neuroblastoma so the only option for Kelli is to go abroad.

The Kelli Smith Appeal which was set up by Kelli's family in September 2011 aimed to raise the £500,000 needed to pay for this and has been a great success. But Kelli and others like her still need your help and so I hope Fairy Boots will go some way towards doing just that.

Enjoy..... and don't stop believing!

All of the author's profits from the sale of this book will go to NCCA UK to help other children like Kelli fight cancer.

The Kelli Smith Appeal is part of a registered charity – NCCA UK (rcn:1135601)

For more details please go to http://thekellismithappeal.com/

Or check out The Kelli Smith Appeal on Facebook.

With a smile that could melt the entire North Pole,
And blue eyes that could reach to the depths of your soul,
Young Kelli was special and right from the start,
She charmed all those who knew her and captured their hearts.

Now Kelli was poorly and though doctors tried,
They just couldn't fix all of the damage inside.
But Kelli kept smiling as much as she could,
Though she found some days hard as most anyone would.

One morning she went to the garden to play,
But before she could get there Mum stood in her way.
"Make sure you have put on a coat and a hat,
You mustn't catch cold now — we wouldn't want that!"

"Be sure to put boots on and lovely warm socks,
They're under the stairs in the big cardboard box.
She opened the cupboard and rummaged around,
But slippers and school shoes were all that she found.

Kelli searched on the shelf 'til her fingertips felt,
What a soft pair of boots! – And an old leather belt.
The belt was her Dads but the boots, which were green,
Were ones which Miss Kelli had not before seen.

She sat on the stairs where she thought for a bit,
Then decided to try them and see if they fit.
She slowly untied them and slid in her feet,
They fit her so perfectly – oh what a treat!

As she did up the laces she heard a voice say,
"That tickles! Now come on – let's be on our way!"
"Who said that?" asked Kelli. The boots they replied.
"Why WE did. Now come on lets go play outside!"

"But where did you come from? You're surely not mine".
They said "We've been waiting a very long time".
"Then how did you get here? I've only just come,
To live in this house with my Dad and my Mum"

"We know that you're poorly and so is your Dad,
We're here to encourage you when you feel bad"
When she asked who had made them, the boots they replied
"We'll show you — they live in the oak tree outside"

Kelli ran down the garden and there in the fence,
Was a door she'd not noticed — it didn't make sense.
"I shall never get through there, because I'm too tall".
Boots answered "Think happy thoughts, then you'll be small!"

"Pasta and pink stuff and lots of ice cream!"
In an instant she shrank – it was just like a dream.
Kelli pushed the door open and tiptoed inside,
Where she gazed all around with her eyes opened wide.

As the leaves spiralled downwards from all of the trees,
Blue fluttering butterflies danced with the bees
It was just like the magical land in her books,
With toadstools and lots of small crannies and nooks.

She carefully took down a lantern to hold,
As she tiptoed through leaves which were red, brown and gold.
Then further and further she carried on going,
Wait! All of a sudden, she saw something glowing.

There sat on a log was a big leather book,
So Kelli sat down for a rest and a look.
It was filled up with poems and stories and spells,
Which were carefully written, by Fairies and Elves.

Just then a red squirrel came down from a tree,
"Why! You must be Miss Kelli – oh good gracious me!"
The fairies are waiting to meet you – let's go!"
I'll show you a short way to get there I know"

She followed the squirrel and came to a pond,
"Please wait" he said kindly — and then he was gone.
Kelli took off her boots and was washing her toes,
As a dragonfly hovered and tickled her nose.

Kelli got a surprise when she turned back around
For the fairies had come without one single sound.
They each had on small jackets with little puffed sleeves,
Which were made out of petals and fresh autumn leaves.

"I'm Finnan. C. Thistleberry Jr — that's me"
Said a handsome young fairy bent down on one knee,
We're so glad you have come here, but ask this I must,
Will you help us? We've lost all our magical dust.

"We buried it so it would stay safe and sound,
But we can't find the place where we dug in the ground.
Alas, without Pixie dust, we cannot fly,
Then the trees will all wither and the flowers will die.

"There must be a spell in that big magic book,
Let's find it" said Kelli "I'll help you — let's look!"
So they searched all the pages as fast as they could,
And then armed with a wand they set off through the wood.

Soon the wand started shining as bright as a star
So they knew that the pixie dust couldn't be far.
Kelli read out the words from the spell they had found,
And before them a hole opened up in the ground.

There it was – all the pixie dust, every last drop,
Which they'd put in a barrel and fastened the top.
So then back to the oak tree they went hand in hand,
With their dust safe and sound what a merry wee band!

"We really can't thank you enough" Finnan said.
"Fairy boots brought me" Kelli said "Thank them instead!"
"Come join us for lunch, won't you stay for a bite"
Begged a fairy named Imogen. D. Shimmersprite.

Willow Glitternut brought her a red toadstool seat,
Molly Mossmuddle served up some sweet tasty treats.
Alfie Winterbuck brewed her a fresh cup of tea,
And the shoemaker came from his workshop to see.

Samuel Thistlefoot wasn't the sociable type,
He preferred to make shoes and to smoke on his pipe.
He wore gloves and an apron which covered his clothes,
And a cap and round specs on the end of his nose.

"Your boots cannot heal you, but will make you smile,
They can take you out walking for mile after mile.
"They will never wear out or get too small for you,
Please take care of them Kelli whatever you do".

Kelli promised and stayed 'til the clock had struck four,
And then it was time to go back through the door.
But not before lots of farewells had been said,
And plans made for when next she got out of her bed.

Then Kelli's new boots took her back to her house,
Where she crept through the hall, then upstairs like a mouse.
When her Dad asked her if she had had a good day
She smiled and said "Yes Dad – in EVERY way".

It's going to be fine now, don't worry – you'll see.
That Cancer's not getting the better of me.
I'm going to be happy and brave and so strong.
And if I get sad it won't be for too long.

Now every day Kelli has reason to smile,
And forget all her troubles — if just for a while.
For you never know who you are going to meet,
When some magical boots find their way to your feet.

Lightning Source UK Ltd.
Milton Keynes UK
UKRC02n2216181016
285609UK00004B/5